The Easter

A Play by CHRISTINE

A dramatic presentation c
ideally to be performed in Chu

The Easter Tree represents three things: the wood of the cross, Christ Himself and, ultimately, all that lives and grows on the earth.

CAST

Men:-   Women:-

1ST DISCIPLE   READER

2ND DISCIPLE   NARRATOR

JOHN   MARY MAGDALEN

PETER   1ST WOMAN

THOMAS   2ND WOMAN

3RD DISCIPLE   ANGEL.

4TH DISCIPLE

5TH DISCIPLE

3 MORE NON-SPEAKING DISCIPLES

CHRIST

COPYRIGHT

We do not ask for any "performing rights" royalties, but remind you that it is illegal to reproduce in print, by typing, writing or photo-copying, any part of this play without the Publisher's written permission.

No permission is needed however, to perform this play, providing that copyright obligations, as listed above, are fulfilled.

ISBN 0 86071 106 4

COSTUME

DISCIPLES: Traditional robes of the time.

READER &
NARRATOR: Long tunics (or ordinary dress).

MARY
MAGADALEN: Long black shawl that covers her head and conceals her dress underneath, which is floral and colourful - (it need not be Eastern dress).

2 WOMEN: Black robes, black shawls over head.

ANGEL: Long white robes, wings.

CHRIST: Long white robes with hood or drapery for the head.

MUSIC

You will find a list of suggested incidental music, all available as recorded music, at the end of the book.

THE EASTER TREE.

SCENE I.

Before dawn on Easter Sunday morning.

(A long table covered with a white cloth; on it a flagon of red wine, chalice, loaf of bread on a plate. Behind the table and leaning forwards towards it, is a large black cross (cardboard?).
10 Disciples sit round the table looking weary and wretched, some asleep on their arms.
"The doors being shut where the Disciples were for fear of the Jews".)

READER: (Reads from Revised Standard Version.)
            Mark, chapter 15, verses 22-27,
              "   "   "   "   33-37,
              "   "   "   "   42-47,
              "   "   16,   "   1.

            (Exit.)

NARRATOR: It is finished.
            Behind doors shut and barred -
            Night's dark shut out, and darker night
            shut in -
            They crouch and watch, and start at sounds,
            Fear and shame for food and drink.

            Wine in the cup has a bitter taste;
            Bread - they do not care to break.

            The day is gone; all is finished;
            To this small room, and smaller tomb,
            diminished.

            (Sits.)

1ST   ) (Stands and looks up at the cross.)
DISCIPLE) They took an axe to a tall, straight tree;
            Felled it to the ground with thirty
            strokes and more.

            Listen! You can hear the sound of its fall.
            Never tree fell so heavily.
            Breath no longer stirs in its leaves,
            Nor sunlight through the branches weaves.
            It seems long ago. Did you hear its fall?

            When the growing tree from the earth is
            gone. It's hard to make it grow again.

2ND   ) (Stands.)
DISCIPLE) In time they set it back in the ground.
            Roots once severed can't be joined.
            They set it back in the ground in time;
            Across its head was fixed a beam.

            The growing tree from the earth once gone.
            It's hard to make it grow again.

            (Both sit. Enter John.)

- 4 -

JOHN: (To the Disciples.)
The cock has crowed; morning must be waking.
His Mother, weary, at last is sleeping;
No longer watching, watching and waiting.

(Bitterly.)
Waiting for what? What might she see?
Life spring again from a hewn tree?
There's no daylight here; no sun overhead.
Let the cock crow - it'll not wake the dead.

(Pause.)
He spoke to me - would you believe it? -
"John behold your mother"; and to her
"behold your son."

After that the sky grew dark as death.
Storm clouds pressed their weight to the earth,
Suffocating with a heavy dread
All that gathered company of the dead.

The darkness was complete; it was finished.

To this dark room, and darker tomb, diminished.

(Sits at table, head in hands.)

(All Disciples gradually fall asleep on their arms, or sit with heads bowed.)

SCENE II.

Still before dawn, out of doors.

(Enter Mary Magdalen. She brings spices to the tomb. She is draped in black and carries ar armful of herbs, grasses and wild flowers. She holds some of them up individually as she refers to them.)

MARY) Grey-leaved olive, fragrant spikenard -
MAGDALEN) Crown round your head.
Bitter aloe, hyssop sweet -
Palms strewn at your feet.
Red and white anemone -
Garden of Gethsemane.

(Pause.)

Flowers of the frankincense -
Divine innocence.
Purple-petalled mandragore -
Precious ointment in a jar.
Wisp of darnel grass.....

(Pause.)

As for man, his days are grass
Where the wind blows; see it pass.

(Exit.)

———

SCENE III.

The room, as before. Dawn.

(Pause, then loud, urgent knocking off stage. Two women, all in black, run down the aisle to the table. Disciples stand in amazement and move to ends of table. The women run to the far side of the table so that they face the audience to speak. Disciples sit at ends of table. The women speak breathlessly and excitedly, in turn.)

1ST WOMAN: We went to the tomb,

2ND WOMAN: In the grey before dawn.

1ST WOMAN: Afraid to be seen;

2ND WOMAN: And the heavy stone -

1ST WOMAN: We couldn't have moved it -

2ND WOMAN: The stone had gone.

1ST WOMAN: And we saw...

2ND WOMAN: We saw...

1ST WOMAN: An angel from Heaven,

2ND WOMAN: An angel in white;

1ST WOMAN: And around him a glow,

2ND WOMAN: Like snow in moonlight,

1ST WOMAN: A gleam, like first daylight -

2ND WOMAN: Though dawn hadn't broken.

1ST WOMAN: He spoke to us then,

2ND WOMAN: Said we were mistaken

1ST WOMAN: To look for the dead:

2ND WOMAN: We must look for the living.

1ST WOMAN: Come with us, run!

2ND WOMAN: As fast as you can,

1ST WOMAN: Come to the tomb.

(Peter and John run with the 2 women up the aisle to the back of the auditorium.)

SCENE IV.

Dawn. Before the tomb.

(Enter Angel. Peter, John and the two women kneel before the angel.)

ANGEL: Do not look in the dry earth,.
In the dust of the ground, in the dark - for death.

As springing water splashes from a fountain
That grass may drink where it flows in the garden,
The Lord of Life is alive, is risen.
Do not look for the dead, but the living!

You will see Him, lovely to the sight
As leafy pools in the parching desert.

(Exit. LIGHTS OFF.)

(Disciples return slowly to the room and table, down centre aisle. Two women return down side aisle and exit.)

SCENE V.

(The Disciples at the table sit up or stand at the return of Peter and John. Peter speaks disjointedly, but emphatically.)

PETER: I am telling you the truth -
You'll scarcely believe it:
There is no death -
Death is defeated -
No need to be afraid;
The night is over.
There's sunlight outside,
It's not dark any more.

JOHN: Open the shutters!
Morning is here.
Let in the daylight,
The morning air.

PETER: The dark has vanished;
He was dead and is living.
An angel has promised

PETER & JOHN: With our own eyes we shall see Him.

(Thomas jumps up and turns his back.)

PETER: Thomas!.

(Thomas turns slowly.)

THOMAS: (Slowly.) I find it hard to believe.
I would like to believe these sayings.
We've felt so numb; it's hard
To feel life flowing back in our veins.

We seemed to die that day.
I think I speak for us all

When I say we ask – why? –
Why did it all fail?

(Pause.)

3RD)   (Stands.)
DISCIPLE)   There is a time to choose the earth,
To wait in the quiet and the gloom,
Till the year leaves Winter's cocoon
And dries its wings in the sun.

4TH)   It's more than that: you'll grant –
DISCIPLE)   Though the earth is not the end –
The seed is not the plant.
What did He intend?

5TH)   Listen! He did say
DISCIPLE)   That He would have to die –
And yet He spoke of banquets,
Of food, wine, guests,
And invitations sent.
Do you see what He meant?

Who follows Him in life and death
Will leave the dust and grief of earth;
Will drink the wine He died to give;
Will die and, dying, live.

(All sit.)

(LIGHTS OFF TABLE.)

SCENE VI.

The Garden.

(The meeting of Mary Magdalen with "the gardener" is mimed with appropriate background music.

Mary Magdalen enters, in black, carrying her herbs and grasses, one hand covering her face: "They have taken away my Lord and I know not where they have laid Him."

Christ enters, in white, head covered. He goes up to Mary and stands still. She gestures despair. He holds out His hands. She recognises Him, kneels, holds out one hand; He holds out one hand towards her, but they do not touch. She gives Him a white flower - their hands do not touch as He takes it.

The Disciples sit and watch, perfectly still.

Christ slowly leaves. Mary slowly rises and steps forward, as if in a trance. Her black drapery falls off to reveal a colourful floral dress underneath. She holds her herbs and flowers in both arms before her and speaks as if in a dream.)

MARY   )   Sing a song of the vineyard,
MAGDALEN)   The growing vine.
                 The gardener tends it;
                 The grapes are sweet as wine.
                 The wine is pressed:
                 Taste it, taste!
                 Sweeter than honey
                 Is the gardener's face.
                 Branches of the vine,
                 Come and see:
                 The grapes are ripening
                 On the vine-tree.

Winter's hand
Has loosed its dark hold
To sap of summer,
Sunlight's gold,
Green of wet grass,
Green of growing leaves.
Corn will be golden
In summer's ripe sheaves.
The grain is roused
From its earthy bed;
In dancing fields
Springs the living bread.

My love was walking
In a garden of flowers;
Soft the earth
After morning showers.
The leaves are green –
Come and see –
The grapes are ripening
On the vine-tree.
Taste the wine –
The grapes are wet with rain.
Sing of the vineyard, a song
Of no more sorrow or pain.

(Exit.)

SCENE VII.

The room.

(Disciples sitting round table, still bewildered. Enter Christ. He walks forward slowly and the Disciples stand as He takes His place, standing at the centre. He gestures to the Disciples to sit in their places, which they do. He holds out his arms to the shape of the cross above Him; then breaks the bread which is on the table and distributes it to the Disciples; then pours the wine and hands round the cup. After this all sit still and silent, as a tableau.)

NARRATOR: There was a seed once hidden in the ground;
It grew into a tree high on a hill.
Its branches stretched out far across the land
And birds came from the air to rest and build.

Roots reached down to drink deep in the earth;
Fruit formed, as bud grew ripe and flower stirred;
Green leaves murmured with air's every breath,
And creeping things and cattle loved their shade.

There was a tree, stark, shorn of branch and leaf,
Raised on a hill outside a city wall -
The virtue of its fruit beyond belief;
Dry wood, that springs with life; a living well.

As mustard grain to tree; good wheat from weed:
So keeps a Kingdom's secret in a seed.

(Sits.)

CHRIST: You have believed, because you have seen me.
Blessed are those who have not seen, yet believe.

(The Disciples do not notice as Christ quietly leaves. Exit Disciples slowly by other ways.)

———————

C U R T A I N.

SUGGESTED INCIDENTAL MUSIC

1. Introduction to the performance.
   Symphony No. 6 by Prokofiev. Largo.
   (Lasting approx. 1½ mins.)

2. Introduction to Schene II.
   Fantasia on a theme by Thomas Tallis by Vaughan Williams.
   (About ½ min. to cover the entry of Mary.)

3. Introduction to Scene IV.
   Symphony No. 5 by Prokofiev, 1st movement.
   (About 20 secs.)

4. Introduction to Scene V.
   Symphony No. 4 by Mahler, 3rd movement.
   (About 1 min. to cover the return of Peter & John to the table.)

5. Introduction to Scene VI.
   Symphony No. 1 by Elgar, 3rd movement.
   (About 2 mins. to last the entire mimed action.)

6. Introduction to Scene VII.
   London Symphony by Vaughan Williams, 2nd movement.
   (About 4 mins. to last the entire mimed action.)

7. Conclusion.
   9th Symphony by Beethoven, 3rd movement.
   (About 1½ mins.)

   In each case the music was "faded in" and "faded out" so that music and voices overlapped without a pause. The lighting and music were synchronised. A polished performance was achieved with 5 rehearsals.

MOORLEY'S are growing Publishers, adding several new titles to our list each year. We also undertake private publications and commissioned works.

Our range of publications includes: **Books of Verse**
- Devotional Poetry
- Recitations
- **Drama**
- Bible Plays
- Sketches
- Nativity Plays
- Passiontide Plays
- Easter Plays
- Demonstrations
- **Resource Books**
- Assembly Material
- Songs & Musicals
- Children's Addresses
- Prayers & Graces
- Daily Readings
- Books for Speakers
- **Activity Books**
- Quizzes
- Puzzles
- Painting Books
- **Daily Readings**
- Church Stationery
- Notice Books
- Cradle Rolls
- Hymn Board Numbers

Please send a S.A.E. (approx 9" x 6") for the current catalogue or consult your local Christian Bookshop who should stock or be able to order our titles.